Indigenous History from 1952–1968

THE TERMINATION ERA

by E. A. Hale

FOCUS READERS
NAVIGATOR

WWW.FOCUSREADERS.COM

Copyright © 2025 by Focus Readers®, Mendota Heights, MN 55120. All rights reserved. No part of this book may be reproduced or utilized in any form or by any means without written permission from the publisher.

Focus Readers is distributed by North Star Editions:
sales@northstareditions.com | 888-417-0195

Produced for Focus Readers by Red Line Editorial.

Content Consultant: Katrina Phillips, PhD, Red Cliff Band of Lake Superior Ojibwe, Associate Professor of History, Macalester College

Photographs ©: AP Images, cover, 1; JM/AP Images, 4–5; Red Line Editorial, 6; National Archives, 9; Keystone/FPG/Archive Photos/Getty Images, 10–11; Bettmann/Getty Images, 13, 15; Susan Montoya Bryan/AP Images, 16–17; Heritage Art/Heritage Images/Hulton Archive/Getty Images, 19; Harry Harris/AP Images, 21; Henry Burroughs/AP Images, 22–23; P143-1010/Alaska State Library/Alaska Dept. of Health & Social Services Photo Collection, 25; US Department of Defense, 27; John Kunkel Small/Library of Congress, 29

Library of Congress Cataloging-in-Publication Data
Library of Congress Cataloging-in-Publication Data is available on the Library of Congress website.

ISBN
979-8-88998-414-6 (hardcover)
979-8-88998-442-9 (paperback)
979-8-88998-494-8 (ebook pdf)
979-8-88998-470-2 (hosted ebook)

Printed in the United States of America
Mankato, MN
012025

ABOUT THE TERMINOLOGY

The terms **American Indians** and **Native Americans** are used interchangeably throughout this book. With more than 570 federally recognized tribes or nations in the United States, the usage will vary. Native nations and their people may use either term. The term **Indigenous peoples** describes groups of people who have lived in an area since prehistory. It may also be used as a shorter term to describe the federal designation **American Indians, Alaska Natives, and Native Hawaiians**.

ABOUT THE AUTHOR

E. A. Hale is a proud member of the Choctaw Nation of Oklahoma.

TABLE OF CONTENTS

CHAPTER 1
Assimilation Through Relocation 5

CHAPTER 2
Terminating Tribes 11

CHAPTER 3
Native Struggles 17

CHAPTER 4
Health and Well-Being 23

VOICES FROM THE PAST
Medicine Man 28

Focus Questions • 30
Glossary • 31
To Learn More • 32
Index • 32

CHAPTER 1

ASSIMILATION THROUGH RELOCATION

Before the 1940s, the US government considered **Indigenous** tribes to be **sovereign nations**. Even so, it still tried to reduce tribal power. One method was **assimilation**. In the 1950s, government policies pushed for assimilation in a new way.

The goal of the assimilation era was for Native people to adopt the lifestyle of mainstream Americans.

The US government's Bureau of Indian Affairs (BIA) began a new program in 1952. It was the Urban Indian Relocation

Program. The BIA said the program would help Native people find jobs in cities.

But the program aimed to assimilate Native people. The program took Native people from their lands and cultures. The government hoped Native people would forget their heritage. It hoped they would lose their connections to their tribes.

Native people could join the program. But then they had to move. They had to leave their rural Native **reservations**. The program funded part of the move. It gave them a one-way bus or train ticket. It promised good city jobs. Many families and young adults chose the program. There were not many jobs on tribal lands.

Some Native people struggled in cities. The program did not have good jobs for them. Some BIA officers said Native people had to find their own jobs. When they did find places to work, the pay was low. People could not find good places to live. They were not paid enough to support basic needs such as food or rent.

The program also did not give Native people money to go home. The BIA wanted them to stay in the cities. But half of the people in the program returned home. They missed their families. They missed their communities and cultures.

Some people stayed in the BIA program. They formed community groups

COME TO DENVER

THE CHANCE OF YOUR LIFETIME !

Good Jobs
- Retail Trade
- Manufacturing
- Government-Federal, State, Local
- Wholesale Trade
- Construction of Buildings, Etc.

Happy Homes
Beautiful Houses

Government posters promoted relocation. By 1960, more than 33,000 Native people had moved.

in big cities. They lived in pan-Indian neighborhoods. People from various tribes lived near one another. They made friends with Native Americans from other tribes. But they often felt the sting of **discrimination**. Their tribal backgrounds made them a minority in a city.

CHAPTER 2

TERMINATING TRIBES

In the 1950s, Congress also passed policies to **terminate** Native nations. These policies would assimilate Native people. In 1953, Congress passed a law to end **federal** recognition of tribes in several states. It stopped providing federal aid to them. Indigenous people could still claim tribal membership.

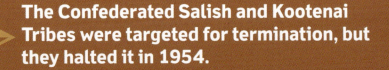

The Confederated Salish and Kootenai Tribes were targeted for termination, but they halted it in 1954.

11

But Congress would not recognize the tribe as a sovereign nation.

The same law closed tribal rolls in these states. No new members could be added. The US government also sold off tribal lands. The money was split among

TERMINATION LIST

From 1953 to 1965, 109 tribes lost federal aid through termination. The Menominee nation of Wisconsin was among the first to be terminated. It owned rich forest lands. Many non-Natives bought the land. Prairie Band Potawatomi Nation was on the termination list, too. Its members fought to keep their status as a sovereign Native nation. They protested. They spoke to Congress. They saved the tribe from termination.

Ada Deer of the Menominee nation led efforts to restore her tribe. She fought against federal policies and won.

tribal members. Tribes lost more than 3 million acres (1.2 million ha).

Congress passed Public Law 280 in 1953. This law gave six states new power. They could handle crimes committed on tribal lands. The law ended federal power to enforce laws on tribal lands. But tribes did not want the states to take their power. This law decreased Native nation sovereignty.

Starting in January 1954, Congress passed more than 40 laws directed at Native nations. Some laws ended the federal status of tribes. However, tribes acted on their own to halt termination laws. Some fought the laws in courts.

The National Congress of American Indians (NCAI) helped, too. It called a meeting in February 1954. People there pressed Congress to stop policies to end tribes. The NCAI asked for workforce training. Then Native people could earn more. The NCAI said these types of actions would decrease the need for aid.

Indigenous people protest assimilation efforts in New York in 1952.

Congress passed Public Law 959 in 1956. It was the Adult Vocational Training Program. Many people called it the Indian Relocation Act. It trained Indigenous people. Thousands of young adults left tribal lands. Some got jobs as nurses, auto mechanics, welders, and office workers.

15

CHAPTER 3

NATIVE STRUGGLES

The Indian Citizenship Act of 1924 said all Native people born in the United States were US citizens. But the US Constitution gave states power to set voting laws. Some states had unfair laws to keep people from voting. For example, a state law could require a voter to have an address. But some people living on

> Miguel Trujillo (right) of the Isleta Pueblo helped win voting rights for Native people in New Mexico.

reservations did not have one. Some Native people did not read English well. But many had to pass a reading test to vote. States stopped these laws over time. In 1962, New Mexico became the last state to let Native people vote.

Some states had poll taxes. These were fees charged to people of all races. Each person had to pay a tax to enter a voting site. Many American Indians did not have funds to pay the tax. Poll taxes were outlawed by the Twenty-Fourth Amendment to the Constitution. This amendment took effect in 1964.

In 1965, Congress passed the Voting Rights Act. It was for people of all

Poll taxes were one of many ways states kept people of color and poor people from voting.

races, not just Native people. The law strengthened voting rights even more. After the Indian Citizenship Act passed, it still took more than 40 years for all states to let Indigenous people vote.

The US government began the Indian Adoption Project in 1958. It became common for government officials to take

19

babies from Indigenous parents. Workers took some children against the mother's will. They pressured other parents to give their children up.

Over time, Native nations lost thousands of children to outside adoptions. Most of these children were sent to live with non-Native parents.

ADOPTION CRISIS

Tribes protested outside adoptions. They fought to keep Native children. In 1960, the Navajo Nation challenged the project. The tribe argued that all adoptions must be approved by its tribal court. The health of each Native child is tied to their culture. It is tied to their tribe and kin.

In 1968, Spirit Lake Dakota people traveled to New York to advocate against non-Native adoption of their children.

Children were sent far away. Their birth families could not stay in touch with them. The project broke children's ties to their tribe and culture. It was another form of assimilation.

CHAPTER 4

HEALTH AND WELL-BEING

Native people often lacked access to health care. This was a big problem on reservations. This issue finally got more attention in the 1950s. In 1955, Congress created the Indian Health Service (IHS). This department was part of the United States Public Health Service (USPHS).

Annie Dodge Wauneka of the Navajo Nation helped improve health conditions for her people.

The IHS sent a report to Congress about poor health care for Native people.

Access to health care was also a problem in remote Alaska. Many Alaska Natives died due to illness. In 1955, the IHS and USPHS took steps to fix this. They sent teams of health workers. The workers fought a lung disease that harmed Native people in Alaska. The illness was called tuberculosis. It was the main cause of death.

In 1957, Congress funded new Native hospitals and clinics on tribal lands. Health clinics were built in remote places. Some sites got new labs and equipment. Those tools helped run health tests.

In the first half of the 1900s, Alaska Natives were hit harder by tuberculosis than most other groups.

Some Native homes did not have sinks or tubs. Some homes did not have flush toilets. Often, they had only an outhouse. In response, Congress passed another law in 1959. The IHS installed plumbing

25

in homes. It made sure the water was safe to drink. The IHS built sites to clean waste from water. This helped improve the quality of life for Native people. They were less likely to get sick from unclean water.

HEALING FROM WAR

In 1964, many Native people enlisted in the Vietnam War (1954–1975). Some joined out of a sense of duty to protect their Native lands. Others joined due to a family history of service. Tribes held military ceremonies for soldiers on their way to war. They celebrated ancient traditions. Tribes also welcomed veterans home from war. They gave comfort to war-weary Native people. Some tribes held rituals to cleanse the soldiers' spirits.

Cleansing rituals moved Native veterans from a state of war to a state of peace. The healing events helped to restore balance.

In 1965, a Community Health Representative (CHR) program began in the IHS. When Native people needed more care, the CHR program bridged the gap. Tribes hired CHRs, such as home health nurses. They helped those who were still weak after leaving hospitals.

> **VOICES FROM THE PAST**

MEDICINE MAN

Josie Billie was a medicine man from the Seminole Tribe of Florida. He lived on the Big Cypress Reservation in the Florida Everglades. Billie was an **herbalist**. He knew which plants helped his people. He was an expert in healing with nature. People who were ill came to see Billie. He made a tea to calm people. He used a variety of plants in the brewed tea.

In 1958, a drug company in Michigan learned of the tea. The company wanted his recipe. They wanted a safe drug to calm people who were very upset.

Billie sold his secret recipe to the company. He got a new house as part of the payment. In an interview, he said, "I get them bottled, I send 'em some more medicine. . . . I make a lot of different kinds of medicine. But he wants my herbal medicine tea."[1]

Josie Billie (right) learned medicine from older Seminole medicine men. He passed this knowledge on to younger generations.

Billie also helped pass down and protect Seminole history and culture. For example, he helped record Seminole music. Billie played many important roles for his tribe.

1. Josie Billie. "Living Legends Collection." *ListenOK*. Oklahoma Oral History Research Program, 6 Nov. 1958. Web. 24 Feb. 2024.

FOCUS QUESTIONS

Write your answers on a separate piece of paper.

1. Write a sentence describing the main idea of Chapter 1.

2. What impact do you think relocation had on Indigenous families? Why?

3. Which Native nation said that all adoptions must be approved by the tribal court?

     A. Menominee nation
     B. Navajo Nation
     C. Seminole Tribe of Florida

4. Which statement shows the need for better health care for Indigenous people?

     A. Indigenous people lived far from hospitals.
     B. Indigenous people relocated to big cities.
     C. Indigenous people lived in healthy communities.

Answer key on page 32.

GLOSSARY

assimilation
The process of shifting to mainstream lifestyles and living like most other Americans.

discrimination
Unfair treatment of others based on who they are or how they look.

federal
Having to do with the top level of government, involving the whole nation rather than just one state.

herbalist
Someone who studies the use of plants for medicine.

Indigenous
Native to a region, or belonging to ancestors who lived in a region before colonists arrived.

reservations
Land set aside by the US government for Native nations.

sovereign nations
Countries that have their own governments and rule themselves.

terminate
To end a Native nation's status as a federally recognized tribe.

TO LEARN MORE

BOOKS

Doerfler, Jill, and Matthew J. Martinez. *Deb Haaland: First Native American Cabinet Secretary*. Minneapolis: Lerner Publications, 2023.

Sorell, Traci. *We Are Still Here! Native American Truths Everyone Should Know*. Watertown, MA: Charlesbridge Publishing, 2021.

Stall-Meadows, Celia. *Dr. Clara Sue Kidwell: Teacher and Mentor*. Durant, OK: Choctaw Cultural Center, 2023.

NOTE TO EDUCATORS

Visit **www.focusreaders.com** to find lesson plans, activities, links, and other resources related to this title.

INDEX

adoption, 19–21
Alaska Natives, 24
assimilation, 5, 7, 11, 21

Billie, Josie, 28–29
Bureau of Indian Affairs (BIA), 6–9

Community Health Representative (CHR), 27

Indian Health Service (IHS), 23–27

Menominee nation, 12

National Congress of American Indians (NCAI), 14

Prairie Band Potawatomi Nation, 12
Public Law 280, 13–14

reservations, 7, 18, 23, 28

Seminole Tribe of Flordia, 28–29

termination, 11–14

urban relocation, 6–9, 15

Vietnam War, 26
voting, 17–19